Tiia Yli-Valkama
Wonders of Love
The Alchemy of Love

AF209270

© 2014 Tiia Yli-Valkama
Kustantaja: BoD – Books on Demand, Helsinki, Suomi
Valmistaja: BoD – Books on Demand, Norderstedt, Saksa
ISBN: 978-952-286-939-5

On the Edge of Universe

I'm looking, I am.

I'm wondering. Is it me?

In here?

What am I doing, how do I be!

Here and now.

Tiny creature, a human

In the enormous Universe

No worries, In a moment!

The happiness of the moment
is when you
forget the time!

The wisdom of the Heart
Thousands of things have been written in the
books,
Those things that matter to me
are important,
I can find them in my core
from the eternal knowledge of the wisdom of
the Heart.
All I need to do is to listen to my Heart!
Simple!

The joy and life of existence
is to enjoy,
be delighted and happy,
to love!
Yourself!

Selfhood

You thought me the noble art of the selfhood
by being selfish by yourself at first.
I thought you were sassy and conceited
that you don't think about others.
In fact I learnt that pure selfhood,
to act as it feels good in your heart
is the best way to act and not to please
others,
yet still be feeling empathy.
Kindness, appreciation, respect.
Because only by listening to your Heart
you can move on in your life.

Anxiety

Oh, how can I let go of the anxiety,
All those churning emotions.
Jealousy, hatred, anger, bitterness.
All those an ancient karma,
by bursting up from the cells it arouses
negative perceptions and emotions.
Accept them gratefully,
hereby they will serve you the most.
By denying the perceptions you suffocate
yourself.
Everything needs to be processed to be able
to be more harmonious in the next moment.
In the end the only thing left is the state of
love.
Unbelievable, yet true.

Myself

I am her,
She's in me
I'm in her.
I can see her in others as well.
Conscious about how many can be expressed
in different things, in people just at the right
moment!
Everything and everyone has its own purpose
and place!
Trust that you are in a right place.

Suddenly you were standing in front of me
We looked at each other.
Are we living in a reality at all.
The Momentum, the Energy
the joyous Wonderment
that glanced in both of our eyes.

We stood next to each other, where it was
good to be.
Yet everything ceases at some point.
Those moments etches in the memory of the
mind.

Bother

Is it real or is it just an illusion created by the
mind!
Because in reality we are mirrors for each
other.
In the end every feeling is a state aroused
from ones inner core.
If some unfortunate incident happens, is the
meaning of it
to awaken one to take a look in one's own
inner core.
The feelings of bother are always signs of
epiphany things,
of yourself.

To you

In the maze of jealousy I give your name.
I scream your name, call you to come to me.
You
My only love.
You are mine – physically, present.
Now and forever.
Alive, living, in this moment!

There is no hunting feeling anymore,
there is only freedom.
Because freedom is the only road
that can lead to the source of serenity,
to the ocean of love.
Where love is endless
the love of your own heart,
that you fulfill.
I am harmonious, I am here.

The moments with you that I get to experience
flees me off to the dreams, oh so high.
The stream of consciousness is nearly going away.
The power so strong, that it is felt in every cell
- Love.

At the same time the world's most frightening feeling,
thus the most wonderful feeling in your whole body.
The feeling of love!
I'm yours!

Like a black shackle which ties below the
surface.
Trying to breathe through a reed pipe.
Getting air a little.
Wanting to get away from the dark place.

There's only one way.
Listen to oneself, one's innermost.
It is the road of freedom, then the limitations
don't limit, obstacles are no more obstacles,
they become possibilities.

Fear

I see the light shimmering
I want to go for it, I want to be close.
I fear.
The fear is welling from inside.
I didn't understand that it was my own fear,
for myself.
I feared who I am.
I feared my own feelings.

All I wanted was to be the best
For everyone, everywhere.
- Forgetting myself.
Pleasing, supposing that others accept me,
While I was pleasing.

I was wrong, merely by not pleasing
Being genuine for oneself,
Others can see who I am.

After that they can start to look at themselves.

Mirror

As mirrors we reflect for each other
Every one of us
- On the Earth

Those words, expressions, feelings
Everything wells from one's own innermost.
We need existing people,
Who reflects our own feelings for us.

So can there be irritation, can there be anger.
If some person causes those feelings,
It is a matter aroused from one's innermost.

A matter which requires your attention, a
matter that
One should start to handle.
I admit, matters are painful.
Sometimes one needs tears and yet more
tears.
But when starting to dare facing one's own
innermost,
It is a journey, the best adventure has begun
To more harmonious life.
To the place where one only feels love and
empathy.

Promises

Hey, you said
You promised
You swore.

Where did those promises stay?
I was mistaken to live in the jungle of
promises.
In the jungle where I was tied in to others
lianas.
From now on I only hold on for
My own lianas.
Because that a way I can rule and control my
own life.

Disappointments

Does disappointment exist?
There is a matter or feeling that I wait for,
I have created expectancy to the future.
How can I create expectancy to the future
if there is only this moment?

The feeling brought by the moment, the
experience,
I will live it fully.

Because fear creates expectancies to the
future,
The wisdom of heart likes the present.

So if I create expectancies to the unexpected
Which can only be defined by the present
There can't be a disappointment.

Expectations are illusion, delusion.
I live in the moment.
I feel better.

Decision

When you decide to do something commit to
your thought, to the decision.
Because then the whole universe is
supporting you
And quivers frequently with you.
As long as you hold on to your own good
feeling!

Wounds are made
To be healed.
Scars can be faded out.
Oneself can be harmonious.

You came
You messed up my world.
You were there
So close yet so far.
I wanted you, only you.
You were on my mind days and nights
All the time.

I let go
Because I understood that one can't seize.
I can't seize, I can't be seized.

What happened?
We are independent of each other.
We are each other, always.
But we don't need each other
Though we need,
Without seizing to each other.

Hand in hand, together,
free.

Bestowing other to experience all, the
experiences
also bestowing oneself to experience all the
experiences.

I want what is best for him.
He wants what is best for me.
We are harmonious.
Together and alone we are strong.

Every time I saw you
You reminded me of something important,
Of myself
Of the love of my own heart.

The wave of your energy brought about
strength
Which ignited inside of me.
By that strength I remembered myself,
I remembered to take care of myself.

Neither words nor touch was needed,
No glance,
Only the energy.
I felt alive.

Tiia

You thought me a lot,
You thought me to live
- For myself.

Selfishness is what one needs
To survive in life.
The noble skill of empathy
Reflects back to oneself.

Yet there existed three rules
Respect, appreciation, love.
Trust is platitude.
By following the precept one can find a lot
Find the most painful spots in one's own
innermost.

You supported, you were there.
I just couldn't sense you nor could you sense
me.

We wanted what was best for each other
At least ostensibly.
Thus we couldn't know what was to be
aroused from the innermost.
What other is going through when
disappearing to the darkness.
A gleam of light can still be seen, the light
fulfilled everything.

Sometimes even though one have thought the direction of life
The plan varies, the mind changes.
The providence of your own heart takes somewhere else.
Always one can't understand, even though
Everything happens to be right.
Nothing can be done wrong, one can only work right.

Everything happens at love.
Everything happens right.
In the state of heart, in that moment, quickly.
You can only be grateful. Grateful of everything.
Thank you for standing by me always.

Those words unspoken
Those feelings unraveled.
Those numerous moments
We were brought together.
We both knew
Not knowing that the other one knew.

We supported each other unconsciously
Through the years
Through the hard times
One after another,
Both on one's own turn.
Sometimes other was strong, other weak
And the other way round.

Not once did we talk.
We only looked in to each other's eyes.

Those looks, those moments,
Did we remember something of ourselves.

Long way has been walked next to each other
It was time to come across
Arouse painful things from innermost
Knowing the power of other's support
- Love.

We arrived to the moment where we met
More closely than ever
Body in a body.
I felt a touch even though I couldn't see you.
I sensed your joy and laughter
Even though I couldn't hear you.

I knew you were there
I felt your love.
We were One.

I harmonized You. You gave me the strength.
We learned a hidden connection.
Whenever, where ever
Knowing the spirit of love.

You heard what I said
Even though I didn't say it out loud.
You sensed the feeling
even though I wasn't present.
You knew when I was feeling down
You knew when I was feeling up.
You felt it all
- By being open to your heart.

I screamed, I shrieked, I raged
In my mind
In my deep innermost.

I cried, I laughed, I was happy
Of every moment
When I understood
All the feelings being aroused
From my own innermost,
No-one else couldn't have been able
To cause them.
No-one can hurt
Because at that moment he tells
His own story about himself,
I have mine.

You came, you went, you were
As you wanted.
I escaped, I became anguished, I learned.
That way I can do it too,
with no excuses.

Why should I explain my existence
somewhere?
Because anyway we are
In a right place at exactly right time.
Everyone can find a moment of happiness
Right there where one is.

Those times, those moments
When I didn't see you
Like you had disappeared,
Even though I knew that the right moment
was upon us.

When I expected the least, you were there.
I saw you from afar
We walked towards each other.
This was the moment we had been waiting for
To see another.

Our eyes met
We stood across each other.
You and Me.
There.
Time stopped.

At that moment we knew
That both of us knew
The alchemy of love
The deepest mien of love
The unity, the presence.
Everything was in that moment.

Interweaving to another
As one.
As spiral.
With every cell, with every sense.
Entering upon the moment.

I wanted, I wanted, I wanted
Everything for me and right now.
Patience.
Virtue.
The homework of one's own path.
One has to process them
Thoroughly
Before getting to the next leg.

Felicity, joy, bliss.
The power of life.
Laughter, giggling, jumping joy.
The elixir of life.

Like a miniature life of my life
A slide
Which keeps streaming.
I met the most wonderful teacher of life at
that moment.

The experiences, feelings, words.
Those all harmonized me.
Anything can't be left inside
Everything needs to be processed.
That is the only way.
Harmonizing way.

Even though you were there, so loving,
So close.

Your tender touch made my every cell to sing.
In the moment.
The thrill of pleasure, the soft surface of the
skin,
Touch, closeness
The feeling which flies you up to the sky.

Entering entirely upon another,
The permission for the body to fly.
To trust to another.

Always so strong, always so sure,
Despite extremely sensitive, receptive and
giving.
In love.

The loss of the stream of consciousness, to
the heights.
Over and over again.
The disappearance of cosmic universe
From that moment.
Only that moment, perfect inflation.

So languid, so good to be.
Close to each other, just the two of us!
Skin next to skin, interweaved to another.
The Kiss
The unbroken bond of eternal union.

Fully under other's spell,
Under one's own good feeling!
Us, there, just the two of us!

Think a second the effects of your words
Think a second the consequences of your
actions.

Rejoice a while of the fun you create.
Enjoy of every moment,
That you bring to your life with your own
creativity.

Life, creativity, fun
Lively
Delighted
The producer of fun.
Alive, by your own luminosity!

The meaning of life
- To live!

Everyone can decide by themselves
How they use their inner feelings in the
moment!
By living, by numbing oneself, by looking other
people's lives,
Or living your own life for yourself,
By creating the most wonderful things in it.
Things, so many things with the only barrier
being your imagination
And yet after that creating fantasies, dreams.
There's no limit, everything is possible,
But first you have to face the hardest thing
To look in your innermost, to listen to your
heart,
Thus everything is possible and there is space
for everything you ever want in your life.

The fire, the power
The strong energy of action.
You easily get scared of it, wanting to vanish.
Every one of us is different and we fulfill
ourselves
By the best possible way, by our own unique
way.
The energy of life beats in every one of us, the
core of love
When we let it out from our heart and let it
shine!
That way we heal the world, before anything
we heal and harmonize ourselves!

You have to enter upon life.
To face your own fears.
To move on.
To rejoice of your own strength
To thank yourself.
You can love unconditionally
From the bottom of your heart.

Where do we need each other,
Since we can't be dependent of each other,
We can't seize to another.
Both of us have the freedom for life, all the
time.

The instance of existence,
As creatures, as humans.
We need touch,
We need closeness,
We need love.

The feeling when your heart is about to burst
Of love to another.
There is the most wonderful and warming
state in your heart
Of love to another, of the feeling of love!

That's where we need each other
To fall in love!
The share love, to give love
And as much as to receive love
With your whole heart!

The monster of jealousy
Which comes up as possessive.
As urge to keep another fully for yourself.
By suffocating another under everyday life,
By taking the freedom of life.
No, that cannot be done.

The will of both, the urge to live
All the time, with every cell.
To sense, to feel, to smell, to see,
To hear, to taste, to sense
Life in every moment.

Soul is neuter
The soul has the freedom
Nobody or nothing can constrain it.
The soul can experience,
To fly, to see, to sense
Whatever it wants.

The state of existence and the fears of old
karmas
Bring negative feelings to life
Of which it's time to let go.

Bestow to another
Before anything for yourself a freedom
To live
Boundlessly

Spiritually!

Without the shackles of bonding,
Because everyone feels life
And the spirit of love,
Which cannot be shackled
It is supposed to fly free!

The deepest meaning of the alchemy of love!

Physically we are still one,
Two together
Physically to feel.
Yet free to experience
Spiritually fly!

You and Me
Here
Just the two of us.
As one.
Me in You
You in Me.

I missed you
I thirsted for you
But only can stay
In the love of your own heart
- Where you can find everything.

You tore me apart
And at the same time you harmonize me.

No, that's not you
That's my own innermost
Which is tearing me apart.
My own fears that I haven't faced,
Which I had to face.
Sometimes it scares me,
But how thankful one is
After facing their own
Deepest fears,
Acknowledged them and let them go.

Now I can love unconditionally,
From the bottom of my heart.

Thank you, that you exist.
Thank you for harmonizing me.

Now I'm yours
Entirely
From the bottom of my heart darling!

Fears
The fear of being left alone
The fear of being dumped
As huge power as love.
To enter upon it,
Being in the rough sea of fears at the same
time
In a rollercoaster.
Trying to dare to love
To trust
Fully.
I'm still afraid.
Insecurity.
What can I do?

To talk
To talk to another
About everything
Feelings, the state of mind, fears, love.

Suddenly you notice that you are still in a void,
In a void which you expect another to fulfill.

Nobody else can fulfill another's void
Everyone has to fulfill it by themselves.
By loving self!
After that one can experience the love for
another with every cell
From the bottom of the heart.

The heart is about to burst
Such a lovely feeling that is.
Fears are faced, they are gone.
There is only the state of love,
The most wonderful feeling in the world.

Love, the feeling that is feared the most,
Because it's deepest aspect includes
Strong fears.
To acknowledge, let the feeling of the fear
exist,
To let go of the fear.
Be grateful.
To love
Fully!
Heart feels only trust
Charming love
Which gets the whole body in to an
unparalleled frequency!
In the good state of love!

I thought I couldn't live without you
I was wrong.
All I need is found in the love of my own
heart.
I love myself, me.
Everything else is more welfare and
More love to my life.
Then the life gets harmonized!

The sympathy of the souls.
Reading the expressions.
The glance of the eyes.
Sincere love, altruistic presence.
Caring about another, concern,
By being truly present.
Everybody together and separately.

It is deeply regenerative power of life
It can't be foretold
It is fully unexpected
It streams in to every cell
It is felt by one's whole presence
It is love!

The core substance of love is to discover
yourself,
After founding yourself, you know the spirit of
love,
The love of your own heart.
You can also love another with your pure
heart.

Consummation
By living for yourself
In the moment
By finding the golden thread of life
The happy medium
Which is good to walk along.
To live for yourself
To love
To enjoy, make the unexpected
The dreams come true!

Consummation – by living.
Encountering another
Whilst he's living for himself.
It is easy to be,
Always in the right place at the right time.
The dissipation of time,
The memorable moments
Always in the different way, thus perfectly
experiencing experiences.
Together all
Everybody together.

You can only be happy
Of every matter
Of every moment
Thankful for yourself
Thankful for another

Thankful for everything.

It is noticed
It is seen
The power of life
Which is welling from the inside
From the deepness of heart.
As love.
For yourself.

Enormous power
The power of love
Between two people
Found each other
Learned to live for themselves
They can only love
Each other and life!

All of that is a consummation!
Experiencing life by every cell
In a pure state of love!
By another fulfilling the life!

Me
My life
The meaning
I'm listening for the guidance
I'm doing my best
Thank you for the opportunity!
Thank you for listening myself!
I, I remember, I'm doing my everything
- With my heart.

Now and always
This moment
My growth and development
I'm ready!

To love life every moment!

The Wonderland of Love

Love is not only
Words and acts
But
An enormous ocean
Of love
Where everything can be found.

The being itself
The joy
Living
Forgiveness
Respect
Appreciation
Trust
The love of your own heart
Association
For yourself
For another
Presence
Silence at the right moment
Listening
In the right time in the right place.

In the Wonderland of Love
Where everything is perfectly
Memorable
Uniquely incredible
To be present for another!
To love another from the bottom of your
heart!